Style Me Vintage®

clothes

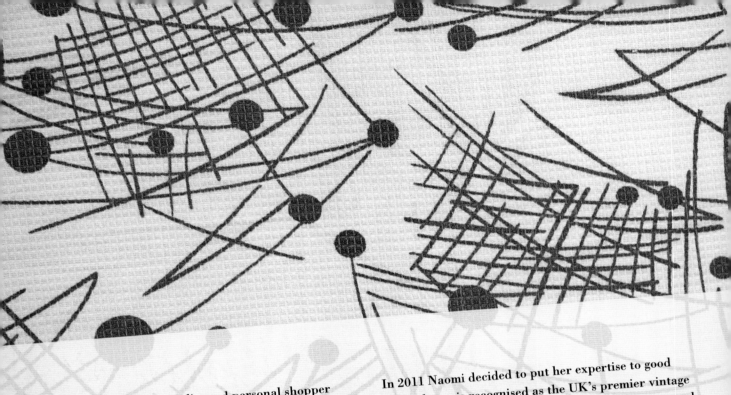

Naomi Thompson is a stylist and personal shopper specialising in vintage fashion. She launched the first high tech on-line vintage shop Vintage Secret, to immediate acknowledgement in the *Guardian's* 'What's Hot' list (second only to Ferragamo), quickly establishing a reputation for sourcing superb quality clothes at reasonable prices.

In 2011 Naomi decided to put her expertise to good use and now is recognised as the UK's premier vintage personal shopper. She is passionate about finding good quality items at the right price, and believes that vintage is the way forward when it comes to creating your own style. Find her at: www.vintagesecret.com

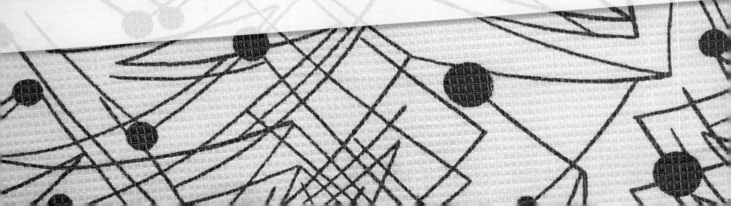

Naomi Thompson

Style Me Vintage®

Easy techniques for creating classic looks

clothes

PAVILION

Contents

Introduction

Have you ever wanted to introduce vintage into your wardrobe, but felt unsure where to start?

Quite often people ask me where I buy my clothes and are surprised when I say, 'It's vintage!' Eschewing 'new' in favour of old, whether on a daily basis or just when you feel like it, is an option open to all and has surprising benefits. Curating your wardrobe from times beyond is like being your own designer and stylist rolled into one. Carefully picking and choosing items allows you to create your very own, unique style. Yes, this can be done with modern clothing, but the palette is limited. I cannot recommend enough the pleasure that comes from going against the grain. Wearing vintage can make you look individual and unique without slavishly following trends or spending money on expensive designer items. The ecological benefits are undeniable. The demand for vintage now means that fewer clothes are being condemned to the rag mill or dumped in landfills.

To help you on your way, you will find an introduction to the styles of the 1920s up to the 1980s. The twentieth century saw the dawn of modern tailoring; no other century has seen such a drastic shift in women's wear. These silhouettes and shapes are still being emulated, and will be for decades to come. You will not find any gimmicky looks here. Each outfit has been carefully selected for its reference points, focusing on a number of factors such as silhouette, print, and hemline, so that you can take this knowledge with you when searching for the perfect vintage outfit. This book does not seek to be a finite textbook guide to the rich tapestry of twentieth-century fashion; instead, it aims to hold your hand and gently guide you in the right direction.

Good classic vintage style is timeless. The looks from these decades are completely wearable today. It doesn't matter if you want to recreate an entire look or mix and match your favourite items from each decade. There is no right or wrong, just lots of fun creating your own vintage style. It may seem daunting at first – but as you build your collection, you will learn what to

look for and what to avoid; and before you know it, you will know what is right for you. Many of my personal shopping clients find that, once they know about vintage cuts and shapes, they discover more about their own shape and find it easier to buy modern clothes.

For me personally, wearing vintage was the natural conclusion of a childhood spent snooping around my maternal grandmother Margaret's house. She was a pioneer of the vintage movement and had been picking up beautiful yet 'unfashionable' cast-offs since the 1960s. My mother and aunties have also worn some of the most cherished items in my collection. Choose your pieces well and they can become heirlooms for generations to come. I love that every dress, every bag, every scarf has a story that it would tell, if only it were able, and that I'm adding a chapter to that story. No modern item has ever made me feel as elegant or unique as a vintage one. Quite simply, vintage has magic. So if, like me, you like to wear clothes to feel creative and expressive, then vintage is for you. I promise that, with a little help, you will be turning heads in no time at all.

Whatever your reason for choosing to wear or explore vintage, I hope this book helps you find that special feeling. Who knows what hidden treasures are still out there to be discovered and enjoyed once more? Don't forget, life is too short for boring clothes.

Naomi

Getting Started

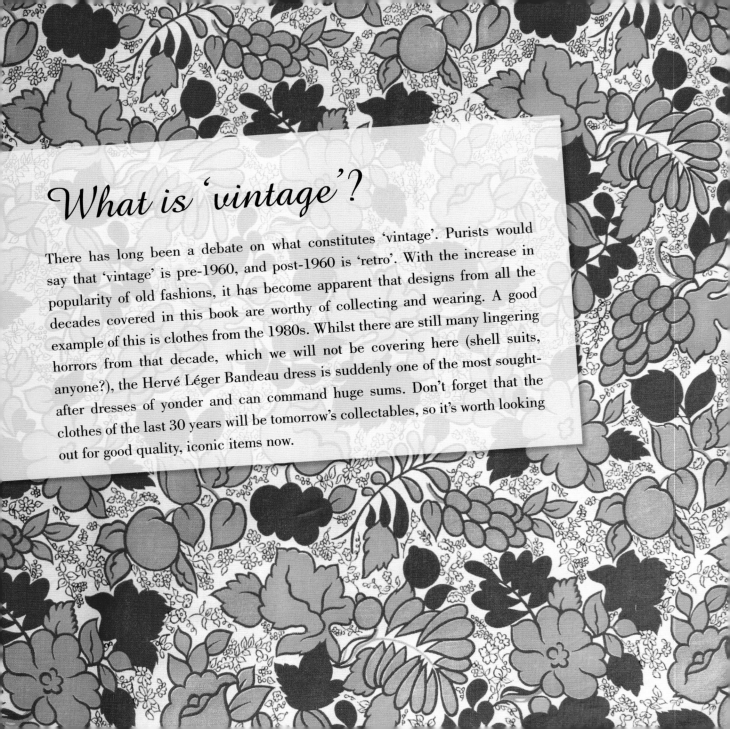

What is 'vintage'?

There has long been a debate on what constitutes 'vintage'. Purists would say that 'vintage' is pre-1960, and post-1960 is 'retro'. With the increase in popularity of old fashions, it has become apparent that designs from all the decades covered in this book are worthy of collecting and wearing. A good example of this is clothes from the 1980s. Whilst there are still many lingering horrors from that decade, which we will not be covering here (shell suits, anyone?), the Hervé Léger Bandeau dress is suddenly one of the most sought-after dresses of yonder and can command huge sums. Don't forget that the clothes of the last 30 years will be tomorrow's collectables, so it's worth looking out for good quality, iconic items now.

11

Quick guide to dating vintage

Learning to date vintage is like learning a language. After a good while of looking at many styles, stitches and patterns, buttons and prints, it just clicks. I promise you it does and is a most satisfying moment. From that point on, you can shop safe in the knowledge that you know what you are buying. Once in a while, an oddity will appear. I once saw a dress with wide tapered bell sleeves and a Celia Birtwell-like pattern. It screamed of the 70s and, in particular, the style of Ossie Clark. All the evidence indicated that it was, in fact, late 1930s. It's an amazing moment when you discover a one-off design that is far before its time. Just imagine the type of gal who would have worn or created such a dress.

There are no hard-and-fast rules for dating vintage, and it is often the source of debate amongst even the most seasoned connoisseurs. It's not uncommon to see a 30s print on a 40s dress, or an older frock with the metal zip replaced. There are always exceptions. It's a combination of the tips opposite and your own developing knowledge that will help to date your finds.

Left: When trying to date vintage clothing, collar shapes and button styles are always a good indicator of era.

1950s and earlier

How does it fasten? Is there a zip? If so, it should be metal. Poppers, hooks and eyes as the only fastener are a good indicator of early 20th century clothing.

Is the label embroidered or in a swirly font? Are the corners folded down where it has been sewn on?

Shoulder pads? Should be small, neat and fairly rigid.

Does it have a bra strap holder? (This is a small poppered ribbon to keep your bra in place between the shoulder and the dress fabric. It is also a sign of quality.)

Has the hem been hand-stitched? Is there a good length of material folded over?

Does it feel old? If it looks too new, it probably is. Trust your instincts.

Post-1950s

Is the zip plastic?

Does it have a care or washing instruction label?

Shoulder pads? May be large, spongy and generally not incorporated.

Does it have a size label?

Is it elasticated?

Have a good look at the inner seams. Are they over-locked? This only became common after the 1960s.

Developing your own style

Don't forget this is about fun! Unless you are trying to be purist, there are no rules. This is not prescribed high street fashion; it's your very own opportunity to build your own style.

When I take people shopping, I never ask their size or age beforehand. There is no need, as I believe that vintage really can be for everyone. You may be looking for a whole new outfit or simply the romance of an old scarf to tie onto a handbag. Please don't think that you are the wrong age or shape. This is not just a young thin woman's game – every age and shape can get in on the scene.

As I said, there are no rules unless you are trying to be a re-enactor – and, frankly, that is not about having fun with your style! Even the most hardcore purists I know like to mix reproduction with genuine vintage, and even the odd bit of high street. There are many good reproduction companies out there – and repro clothes and shoes also feature in this book.

So with that in mind, do remember: the iconic look of one decade quite often followed in to the next as the trends of the younger generations trickled down and became mainstream. Fashions always come in cycles. In the 60s, there was a 20s revival, which can be seen in the short layered dresses and Lolita-like styles. In the 70s, there was a trend for 30s cuts. In the 80s, the 40s can be seen in the resurrection of peplums and shoulder pads. Equally the

"Now is the most exciting time in fashion. Women are controlling their destiny now, the consumer is more knowledgeable, and I have to be better every single day." Oscar de la Renta

50s was back in fashion that same decade with full skirts and large florals. As Celia Birtwell once said, 'Nothing is new, really.'

Laver's Law of Fashionable Design (developed by noted costume historian James Laver) illustrates quite nicely why certain trends and fashion come back around. In fact, it has almost been 50 years since the first ever trend for 'vintage clothing' as we know it.

Laver's Law

10 years before – indecent
5 years before – shameless
One year before – daring
In fashion – smart
One year after – dowdy
10 years after – hideous
20 years after – ridiculous
30 years after – amusing
50 years after – quaint
70 years after – charming
100 years after – romantic
150 years after – beautiful

Never throw out a classic
(this list is according to my grandmother Margaret)

Polka dots

Leopard print

Tartan

Tweed

"The truly fashionable are beyond fashion." Cecil Beaton

Top tips for buying vintage

'Vintage' for me does exactly what it says on the tin. It's not just old or second-hand but a synonym for quality and durability – which may sound a little boring, but these are important factors when buying vintage from which you actually want to get some wear. It's very easy to fall in love with a shape or pattern and feel the need to snap it up instantly, but remember to take a deep breath, contain the excitement, and make sure you follow these essential tips when buying vintage clothes.

• Be prepared. Arm yourself with garments that are easy to get out of; something you can slip on and off without fuss – my favourite uniform for vintage shopping is a button-down dress. Wear minimal make-up. Many vintage garments do up at the side and have to go over your head, rather than over your hips, so whilst its tempting to don a red lippy to get into the spirit of things, it's best not to smear it all over the neck of a yellow 50s frock. You won't be judged in a shop for not looking the part.

• Always hold garments up to the light. Have you noticed how dark vintage shops can be? Well, it's not always intentional (they can just be cluttered places), but it sure does make it harder to spot flaws. By holding it up to the light you can instantly see any holes or repairs. The light will also shine through any patches where the fabric has become too thin and delicate. With woolen garments, check the elbows to make sure there is not excessive wear.

• Always check the armpits. As far as I am concerned, this is Number One in terms of importance; I don't know why it took me so long to do this automatically! Before the days of deodorant, sweat had a habit of damaging fabric due to the acidic qualities of perspiration. They may say horses sweat and ladies glow, but I have seen some amazing dresses (at amazing prices) ruined by sweat marks. Bad examples have a yellowy-green tinge. It can also cause the fabric to shred or a pattern to fade. Some dresses contain built-in sweat pads, similar to a shoulder pad; these can be easily removed without changing the shape of a garment.

- Look at the fastenings. Double-check that none of the buttons are missing and the zips are working properly. This may seem like a no-brainer, but all too often I've gotten home only to discover that a crucial covered button has fallen off or a zip is faulty. Key areas to check fastenings are around the neck line where small buttons may be hidden under a collar, and also around the cuffs. Whilst you are there, make sure the belt is still attached. If there are belt loops and no belt, it's OK to ask for a small discount because the garment is no longer complete.

- Shop with your hands. The best indicator of the quality of a garment is how it feels: is it silk or a bobbly synthetic? Is the twill soft or rough? This will help you identify the difference in quality between two similar dresses or suits of the same cut.

- Talk to the sales assistants. Don't be too proud to ask for advice in a shop, especially if you are looking for era-specific garments. This will speed up the learning process and before long you will be having a friendly debate on the age of a frock. Good shopkeepers should know their stock inside out and quite often they will keep special pieces behind for the right customer. It's also good to develop a relationship with the vendor, as they will start to look out for garments in your size and style. Most vintage sellers are passionate about what they do and are happy to talk to customers about stock, sizes and fair pricing.

- Go for the best you can afford. Resist the temptation to buy in bulk. Despite years of collecting for the sake of it, I now wish I had stuck to buying garments that were 100% wearable and in my size. My repairs bag is huge and you can't 'rescue' everything. The less you buy, the more you can spend on those show-stopping items!

• Shop for your body. Buy garments that fit, that you can move in, and don't be tempted to try and pour yourself into something too small. Whilst shapewear can make a difference (see page 94), you will only end up damaging the garment by splitting the fabric or popping the zip. Style and elegance is not about being a size 8; it is first and foremost about looking fabulous!

• Don't pay any attention to sizes on labels. Sizing is completely different nowadays, and if there is a size label I'm afraid the best option is to ignore it. To give you an example, I am an 8 but fit an 80s 10, a 60s/70s 12 and a 50s 14. Now, is this because women were smaller or are current brands changing sizes to make us feel better about ourselves? This has not yet been answered, and if you are interested in finding out more read up on Vanity Sizing. Gemma Seager, who writes the Retro Chick blog, is considered to be the industry expert.

• Always check the bottom of shoes. More often than not, a heel tip will be missing. Check the leather around the buckle and strap for signs of wear and tear. If a leather strap looks cracked, it may break off easily. Make sure the shoe is not too bendy and will hold your weight – this can be achieved only by trying it on. In some cases the shoe's sole can be reinforced, but this can be costly. Avoid shoes where the leather has stiffened, as they will be uncomfortable to wear.

• Don't be tempted by garments that need altering above and beyond a simple strap shortening or a dropped hem. Scant few alteration shops will do it justice and if the fabric is raw, frayed or thin, it may not last even one cold wash!

• Try to avoid buying items that are 'on trend'. I guarantee that you will be paying more than the item is worth. You will be buying into a fad at an inflated price that will lose its value next season. Buy what *you* like.

• *Don't* be scared to try anything on. If you like it on the hanger, then chances are you will like it on you, but you also shouldn't shy away from the bizarre; sometimes a hanger can't convey an item's true potential, so get it on your body – what's the worst that could happen? As a vintage personal shopper, this has been the most rewarding element of what I do. If I got a pound every time a customer reluctantly tried on a garment which turned out to be amazing, then I could probably retire! Have fun, expect the unexpected and shop with an open mind, as you never know what may turn up.

Vintage Shopping Kit List

A tape measure. With this and a good knowledge of your own measurements, you will save yourself a lot of stress finding changing rooms and squeezing into and out of too small items.

A wide belt to try things on with – dresses can look completely different once they are synched in.

A handbag with a strap to help free up your hands and avoid having to put things down. (I've put things down before, not realised and then seen them sporting a price tag on my next visit!)

A smile – it helps with discounts!

The Looks

The 1920s

"Fashion is not something that exists in dresses only. Fashion is in the sky, in the street, fashion has to do with ideas, the way we live, what is happening." Coco Chanel

The 1920s saw the dawn of style over dictated fashion. The end of the First World War in 1918 brought with it changes that liberated women and led them to rebel against the restrictions of corsetry and modest Edwardian values. Clothing became functional; silhouettes were less exaggerated, yet retained sophistication. As the 20s progressed hemlines crept up to the knee for the first time in history.

Day look shopping list

- Dropped waist lines
- Cloche hats
- Lace-up ankle boots
- Narrow pleated skirts
- Simple jersey knits
- Coloured opaque stockings
- Long tie-collars
- Calf-length hemlines
- Wrapover coats that secure with a single fastening
- Rounded shoes

Evening look shopping list

- Long ropes of pearls or glass beads
- Sheer, often sequinned dresses
- Enamelled or gilded chain-mail bags
- Seed pearl clutches
- Handkerchief hemlines (shorter linings and longer sheer overskirts)
- Bare gloveless arms
- Flesh and soft pastel stockings
- Ornate shoes with Louis heels
- Exotic headdresses and headbands

Main shapes, looks and influences

During the war of the preceeding decade many women had taken up work, and clothing changed to afford greater practicality. Women vastly outnumbered men, and attitudes changed completely from 'dutiful' to 'laissez faire'. The atrocities of war had given people a sense of mortality. Living for the moment became the lifestyle choice of this decade.

Whereas before the 20s the emphasis had been on minimising the waist and accentuating the cleavage, women were now inclined to wear unstructured, shorter dresses that skimmed the hips and flattened the chest. This silhouette is applicable throughout the 20s, for both day and eveningwear. The look was a sleek and slender silhouette, quite flat and boyish. The drop waist was the main feature of the 20s and created a longer less feminine frame. Sashes were popular on day dresses and could be worn loosely around the hips or draped over the shoulder (see page 29). The big revolution, however, was that a visible ankle was now not only socially acceptable but fashionable.

As dress shapes became simpler so did the manufacturing process. Butterick, the pattern company launched in 1863, introduced the first pattern instruction sheet, 'the Deltor', which removed the need to be an experienced dressmaker. This, combined with simple shapes, enabled women to make their own clothes. Designer patterns became popular in women's magazines, often emulating Chanel or Lanvin designs. These garments were also easier to wash and repair.

Coats buttoned up really low, often with one single fastening. Opera coats became popular, but the big trend was a velvet Devoré evening coat, trimmed with luxurious fur such as mink or sable.

Hats changed from wide-brimmed floral extravaganzas to daintier cloches and smaller hats to fit in with the new streamlined silhouette.

The opening of Tutankhamen's tomb launched Egyptomania, especially in accessories. Handbags, shoes and cigarette cases were all adored with the hieroglyphics discovered in 1923. Chain-mail bags peaked in popularity in the Edwardian era and were used throughout the 20s. Seed pearl bags were all the rage and featured a small side strap, commonly thought to be for slipping your hand though, but which was, in fact, to secure your gloves. This was then carried much like a clutch.

Coco Chanel designed her little black dress in 1926, known as the 'Model T' after Henry Ford's popular car. She was arguably the most important influence of this decade. At the forefront of female emancipation, she introduced simply cut garments influenced by men's designs, such as wide trousers (though still very avant-garde for women), long jumpers and, crucially, women's tailoring.

Far left: Velvet opera coat with balloon sleeves in a geometric print.

Above left: Boudoir dolls were reportedly used as a fashion accessory by those who sought to emulate the childlike look.

Above right: A selection of cloche hats and ornate hat pins.

25

Below: Earlier accessories can still complete a 20s look, such as hair combs and mesh bags.

Right: 'Modern' accessories of the day included celluloid arm bangles and seed pearl clutch bags.

Opposite: This 20s dress is relatively long but has a daring side-split.

Top 20s tip
Avoid the clichéd look of long gloves and a hair feather and instead go for a simple gold head band draped around the forehead and metres of looped glass beads.

What was new?

As the decade progressed a new poster girl for excess and indulgence emerged around 1926: The Flapper. The term 'flapper' has roots going right back to the 17th century and referred to a young and vivacious girl. The 1920 film *The Flapper* bought the word into popular culture. The name reflected a somewhat juvenile desire not to grow up. This gal was all about all having fun: drinking, smoking, misbehaving in public and dancing outrageously until the small hours. To go with this brazen behaviour, Flapper attire was more revealing than ever before in history. Dresses were generally sleeveless and fabrics were so fine they bordered on sheer. They were usually lavishly embroidered with sequins and glass beads. Few have survived today as the early sequin was made of gelatine, which had a tendency to melt. Towards the end of the 20s, the streamlined silhouette remained but the detailing became simpler.

It was at this point in the mid-20s (and not before) that the knee briefly appeared. Hemlines were shorter than ever and often trimmed with rows of beaded tassels. There is much debate about how much knee was actually shown. This depended on the cut of the dress: some fell below the knee, but exposed the thigh by a side-split, others just skimmed the knee.

Flamboyant use of make-up added to the Lolita effect: heavy ringed eye make-up, doll-like eyebrows, and scarlet lipstick on a pale face. Hair also underwent a dramatic transformation.

Whilst it was still popular to have it curled and pinned up, a new shorter style appeared: the Bob. This boyish crop symbolised the cutting away of Edwardian sensibilities. Finger waves were also popular and could be combined with a new shorter 'do.

The combination of childish innocence and open sexuality caused scandal amongst the establishment. The Flappers didn't really care; this was the Jazz age and and they were determined to celebrate their own youth.

Informal Looks

On the right, Teowa is wearing a drop-waisted 20s day dress with a shoulder sash (this could also be worn as a loose belt). Note the pleated skirt and embroidered detailing. She is also wearing typical 20s satin court shoes edged in gold leather. The black dress on the left shows a style that would have been worn by an older woman. It follows the fashionable straight lines and pleats of the decade, but is less risqué.

A Flapper Look

Annie is wearing a 20s gold sequinned evening dress. The shoulder straps consist of strands of glass beads and the side slits are are decorated with tasselled roundels. This sandal style of shoe was more popular in the 30s, but can be made to work with a 20s outfit. A classic 20s shoe would have had been similar, but with a closed toe. The look is finished off by celluloid arm bangles, an ostrich feather hair piece and a late Edwardian chain bag.

The 1930s

"When a woman smiles, then her dress should smile too."

Madame Vionnet

The 1930s saw the beginning of social unrest on both sides of the pond. The Great Depression hit the United States and World War II started in Europe. Cinema provided much-needed escapism. The gamine playfulness of the last decade was pushed aside and a new age of strong feminine dressing swept in. Clothes became even more practical, in the form of well-tailored suits, or they became outrageously glamorous as epitomised by the sirens of the silver screen. The clothes of the 30s were cut to suit the female body: instead of trying to change the silhouette, they celebrated the female physique. Curves were definitely back in fashion.

Day look shopping list

- Calf-length hemlines
- Gored, A-line skirts (flaring panels)
- Shawl collars
- Top-stitching, contrast fabric insertions, large buttons.
- Neckline details such as a pleated yoke, ruffled jabot, bow or Peter Pan collar done up high
- Cap or puff sleeves
- Tilt hats – worn tipped to the side and adorned by bows, feathers or brooches
- Muted earthy tones of mustard, jade and reddish brown
- T-bar stacked heels
- Lace-up ankle shoes with a rounded toe
- Wide-brimmed straw hats with a low crown (for summer)

Evening look shopping list

- Full length, cut on the bias and draped
- Dark velvets in jewel tones
- Deep V-necks, front and back
- Full-length skirts
- Scalloped edges
- Fishtail skirts
- Matching or integral belts with a carved celluloid or paste clasp
- Art Deco cut jewels
- Jackets with a nod to Leg o' Mutton sleeves

Main shapes, looks and influences

The general look for both day and evening was sleek. Day skirts and dresses often included pleated or inserted panels called godets, starting below the knee or just above the hemline. The emphasis was on detail, such as buttons, lace, bows. Utter chic and femininity was combined with functionality and simplicity.

This decade also saw the first widespread use of regenerated fibres such as rayon, which was first known as art silk. It was used as a cheaper substitute for both day and eveningwear.

By the mid-1930s, empire lines became popular accompanied by short jackets or capelets. Dresses were cut with a fitted yoke and a strong emphasis on the shoulders, which paved the way for the shoulder pads of the 1940s. The print that epitomises this era for me is floral pastels contrasted with black, for both day and evening wear.

Evening dresses became quite daring. Some were made to be worn bra-less, such as Molyneux's trend for white backless slip dresses, a look completed by a fur draped over the shoulders, or a velvet Opera coat with a fur trim.

The sandal as we know it appeared in the 30s. Ferregamo, shoe maker to the stars, invented the wedge heel in 1936 to combine comfort and style. The T-bar was popular for day and evening shoes. Evening shoes were often made of satin, trimmed with silver or gold kid leather, and accented with rhinestone buckles.

What is a bias cut?

The 'bias' cut is first and foremost a dressmaking technique that involves cutting the fabric against the grain. A bias cut dress is quite often characterised by V-shape panels below the bust line.

So how is it done? The pattern pieces are first cut against the grain and then sewn across the grain of the fabric. This allows it to drape elegantly whatever your shape or size. This is a clever trick to give horizontal stretch to inelastic fabrics. It flatters and enhances the contours of one's physique without being too tight and appearing lumpy. This cut is often accompanied by a long skirt for a beautiful willowy look.

Above: Housecoats/dresses became popular in the 30s for the middle classes and would be worn for lounging, not cleaning, as is often the misconception. Far from being dowdy, they were beautifully made as outerwear. Kezia is wearing a housedress with Greek key motif and 'fruit salad' coloured glass earrings.

Far Left: Gemma is wearing an early 1930s calf-length silk dress with a large bow-effect collar, balloon sleeves and cummerbund-style belt. Its straight cut with smooth lines creates a long, lean silhouette.

Three influential designers of the 30s were Coco Chanel (again), Vionnet and Elsa Schiaparelli. Madame Vionnet, who had trained at the famed Callot Soeurs couture house in Paris, was responsible for many of the well known shapes that are associated with eveningwear of the 1930s. She was renowned for her drapery and popularised halter necks and the bias cut.

The art of Surrealism extended its influence into the worlds of textiles, fashion and interiors. Schiaparelli collaborated with many of her friends, including Salvador Dali, basing her humorous inventions, such as the Tear Dress, on their work. This went against the grain of 'grown-up' fashions. She also invented Shocking Pink and her tailoring was an antidote to the formality and drapery of Madame Vionnet.

What was new?

Sportswear slowly crept in via Chanel in the late 1920s, but became fashionable in its own right in the 1930s. Lacoste began in 1933 and Fred Perry shot to fame in the 1930s with his consecutive Wimbledon wins. The 30s in general promoted 'the body beautiful' and a toned and lean shape. Exercise activities, such as group aerobics, were encouraged. Swimming, tennis and cycling were also hugely popular and clothing ranges were developed with this in mind. Holiday time for workers became a mandatory requirement, which meant beach holidays increased in popularity. Play suits, pyjama suits and all sorts of novel leisurewear inventions were seen on the sandy shores of Britain.

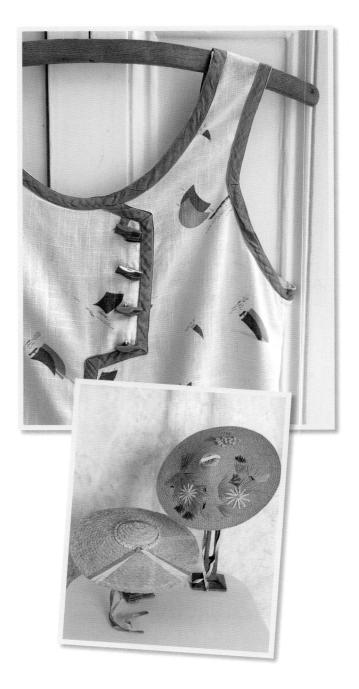

Top tip to date a 1930s dress

Take a good look at the fastenings. Zips were not commonly used in women's wear as they were considered unreliable, and therefore prone to immodesty. Dresses mainly fastened via hooks and eyes, or poppers (press studs), on the side seam, or via rouleau loops and small covered buttons down the back.

Near right: Pairs of deco clips were used for shoes and dresses and could be mounted as brooches. Crocheted gloves were easy to make at home.

Far right: Celluloid diamante brooches were popular accessories. Country pursuits influenced daytime accessories as seen in this duck brooch and glass bird necklace.

Opposite top: Leisure- and sportswear became popular in the 30s, as seen in this beach dress with sailing motif and early plastic toggle buttons.

Opposite below: Low-brimmed 30s straw hats with ribbon ties.

Daytime Look

Gemma is wearing a repro-1930s suit from Puttin' on the Ritz with asymmetric pleat detailing on the skirt and a curved collar to the jacket. The skirt is a classic mid-calf-length. On the jacket there's a single button fastening, which was very in vogue. The original 1930s blouse is made from rayon crêpe, in chocolate brown with orange print, and features a 'jabot' (neck ruffle) with a Bakelite button. Her outfit is finished off with a felt hat and glacé leather gloves.

Evening Look

Kezia is wearing a full length, satin back crêpe evening dress, cut on the bias with a shirred bodice and waterfall beading. She carries an ostrich feather fan and white faux fox stole, and long elegant silver cigarette holder. Smoking was socially acceptable, and even encouraged. Although we cannot see it from this angle, the dress features a low V-back, which is very characteristic of a 30s evening look.

The 1940s

"Nothing is so dangerous as being too modern; one is apt to grow old-fashioned quite suddenly." Oscar Wilde

By the 1940s, war had broken out across Europe. Fashion was no longer the primary concern, but standards were there to be maintained. Raw materials such as cloth were in short supply and much of the traditional labour had left to fight. Rather than buying 'new', women were encouraged to 'make do and mend'. Many shapes of the 30s were simplified to suit the demands of the times. Whilst fabric was in short supply, necks and backs were covered up and modesty prevailed once more.

Day look shopping list

- Tweed
- Headscarves
- Chunky synthetic jewellery
- Peplums
- Seamed stockings
- Single-breasted jackets
- Shoulder pads
- Housecoats, aprons and pinnies
- Mah-Jong bracelets
- Suits

Evening look shopping list

- Most evening dresses were adapted from pre-war dresses, so there is a genuine crossover in styles
- Platform-soled shoes with or without a peep toe
- Crêpe dresses
- Cordé bags
- Carved Bakelite jewellery
- Furs

Main shapes, looks and influences

A typical wartime look was a prim dark crêpe dress adorned by whatever pretty embellishments were available. Wartime garments tend to be darker and less patterned, as people refashioned old fabrics by dyeing them. Sequins came under the Utility Scheme and Civilian Clothing Order, which forbade their use. Even if these rulings hadn't been in place they would have been hugely difficult to get hold of as the best makers were in occupied Europe. There are still some examples of utility clothing which are embroidered with sequins. There is evidence that the ruling was relaxed later on in the decade, which is why some sequin-embellished garments are seen bearing the CC41 label.

It wasn't all doom and gloom. British clothing company Jacqmar was producing bright propaganda scarves as a morale-boosting exercise, and the US continued to manufacture brightly coloured printed garments such as Swirl pinafore dresses, which were favoured by housewives.

This was the decade that trousers became acceptable, even featuring on the front cover of US *Vogue* in May 1941! Initially adopted by women working in factories, they were practical, which made them a desirable garment. High-waisted and wide-legged, they were often described as slacks.

Unlike other clothing, hats were not rationed, though snoods and head scarves became very popular as they combined the key themes of the 40s: fashion and practicality.

The signature 40s look of narrow hips and wide shoulders can be seen on Lisa on page 49. Suits shifted to a boxier jacket with less fabric in the length. The shoulder was lengthened by the arrival of the mighty shoulder pad (not an 80s invention as many still think).

Left: Fleur is wearing Heyday swing trousers, a hand-knitted-from-vintage-pattern bolero, a Heyday Olivia blouse and white Re-mix vintage wedges, finished off with a mah-jong bracelet and a white snood.

Opposite: Cordé bags are very collectable. Suede peep-toe wedges can work well for a day or evening look.

Above left: A stocking repair kit. Stockings were popular but scarce. American GIs would bring with them highly sought-after nylons, but in the absence of anything better, gravy browning was applied to the legs and a seam was pencilled on to replicate a fully fashioned stocking.

Above right: A UK Utility label, designed by Reginald Shipps, resembled two opened-mouth Pac Men.

Right: Hats were not rationed during the war though many were adapted from much older styles.

Far right: Embellishments were often recycled from the 30s.

What was new?

In 1941 rationing was introduced to the UK. Rather than restricting the distribution of clothing, the aim was to ensure equal access to goods and products. All new clothing produced had to be purchased with coupons. The Utility label was a sign of government-approved quality. Not all clothing was Utility, but all manufacturers were expected to follow austerity measures. The point was practicality. This stamped its mark on fashions of the decade, as shapes changed in accordance with ration allowances. Jackets became shorter and boxier, and often lacked a collar or pockets to save on materials. Hemlines rose to the knee (but not above), buttons went down to 2 or 3 and pleats were definitely out in the UK. The less raw materials used, the better. Utilitywares were hard wearing items, built to last and appeared in a surprising number of ranges and colours. It continued throughout the decade, ending only in 1952.

The fashion houses of Paris launched into production once more in 1945 at the end of the war and a new era of long overdue creativity sprang into life. The mundane came to a sharp end with the unveiling of Christian Dior's ultra-feminine first collection in 1947. Declared by *Harpers Bazaar's* Carmel Snow as 'the New Look' (it was actually called the Corolle Line), it featured the iconic Bar suit, which went on to develop the look of the 50s. During the war, fashion had pretty much stood still. Clothing now became a pleasure once again.

Top 40s tip
For a really authentic 40s look, unearth a patriotic flag brooch or propaganda scarf. Many countries produced their own.

Formal Look

Lisa is wearing a late-40s shantung-effect suit with diamanté button detail and a Hattie Carnegie early-40s sculptural velvet hat with velvet-tipped hat pin. She also wears 40s screw-back black enamel and diamante earings, black suede with rosette detail shoes and a black suede bag.

Informal Look

Fleur is wearing a vintage novelty print Swirl wrap dress, red shoes from Re-mix Vintage Shoes, What Katie Did seamed stockings and plenty of vintage bangles.

The 1950s

"Be daring, be different, be impractical, be anything that will assert integrity of purpose and imaginative vision against the play-it-safers, the creatures of the commonplace, the slaves of the ordinary." Cecil Beaton

The 1950s was a decade of reawakening, rebellion, discovery and progress. Musical genres of the previous decade morphed into new crazes, including doo-wop, bebop, cool jazz, blues and notably the emergence of Rock 'n' Roll; a musical genre that would probably produce some of the greatest icons of the decade or, even, century. In Movie Land, Marilyn gave us curves, and the rebirth of European cinema after the oppression of the war brought us smouldering sirens like Sophia Loren. The shape of the 50s was the contrast of a tiny waist with rounded hips in a pencil or a full skirt. This was truly the decade of the hourglass figure.

Horrockses

Day look shopping list
- Beaded cardigans
- Nipped-in waistlines
- ¾-length sleeves on jackets
- Shelf busts (darted bust lines)
- Cat's eye sunglasses
- Novelty prints and jewellery
- Box handbags
- Bright floral patterns
- Circle skirts
- Tie blouses
- Bobby socks
- Saddle shoes
- Short gloves

Evening look shopping list
- Full skirts
- Long gloves
- Brocade
- Modern synthetics
- Triple rows of pearls, worn choker-style
- Rhinestone paste clip-on earings
- Boned strapless bodices
- Chiffon/Organza
- Layers of petticoats
- Small clutch bags with ornate clasps
- Fur stole or wrap

Main shapes, looks and influences

The 1950s was a time of immense change. Europe was recovering from the devastating effects of World War II with rationing continuing into the early 50s. The world saw great shifts in political attitudes, with the growing threat of communism, fear of nuclear weapons and the Korean War. Great advances in technology saw the beginnings of the Space Race and the Atomic Era, both strong influences on design. For the first time, popular culture focused on 'teenagers', a new subculture whose fashion styles, music choices and cultural influences dominated the decade.

The style associated with the 50s began with Dior's Corolle Line of 1947. The look was characterised by a structured jacket, tiny waist and full skirt. This came to represent the iconic feminine shape of the 1950s. Even today this silhouette is much copied. The shape continued to be worn throughout the 1950s and into the early 1960s, within the framework of dresses and coats alike. Think big belted jackets, and shirtwaster dresses with a full skirt and big collar.

Magazines mixed photography with traditional sketches. It was the dawn of the golden age of fashion photography. For the first time, fashion photographers became stars.

Another great introduction during this era, and what I believe to be one of the most important of the century, is the wearing of jeans and denim as a casual and acceptable daytime look for

men and women. Jeans were first worn in the early twentieth century but only as sturdy work wear. No respectable, well-dressed individual would be seen in them outside of this context. This changed with their rebirth as a fashion staple in the 1950s. Seen as a rebellious item – think James Dean or Teddy Girls – they made a statement and have continued to play a large part in our wardrobes today. To create a 50s look, go for indigo denim with a high waist and turn-ups.

What I love about the 1950s is the bold and fantastic use of print. Fabric designers, such as Lucienne Day and Marian Mahler, had begun to use the most fabulous shapes and colours in textile production. Novelty prints abounded (see fabric on pages 92–3). In the United States, dachshunds and poodles were embroidered and printed onto fabrics. Globally, designs were influenced by the positive attitude towards the future of atomic energy and were widely used in clothing and homeware design.

Horrockses became one of the most respected and iconic companies of the decade, creating beautiful full-skirted frocks in a variety of coloured fruits, flowers and blooms.

The Festival of Britain in 1951 was a celebration of British Design and provided a showcase of post-war recovery. The design styles exhibited were the starting block for a decade of iconic design.

Above: Two examples of the poodle trend.

Opposite: Rachel is wearing a nautical cotton two-piece with a tapered bodice which sits over the skirt. Large pockets with a button detail are quite common on 50s frocks and reflect the increased availability of fabric. Jeni is wearing a pink candy-striped halterneck with a matching bolero jacket.

Souvenirwear and novelty jewellery were popular in the 50s. This painted basket bag would have come from Mexico. The box bag below, although Californian, depicts a scene from the springs of Mount Fuji. Cat's eye sunglasses came in many colours.

In the United Kingdom, Queen Elizabeth II was a source of inspiration for women. She was the first young monarch since Queen Victoria, and her ladylike style was copied up and down the country by women of all backgrounds. Her outfits were always finished with a brooch, gloves and bag.

Lucite became a popular material for the creation of the fashionable box-style handbags. These small, translucent creations were luxurious and expensive, but cheaper designs soon came onto the market.

Lucite was also a popular material for sexy, see-through shoes. The heel of these would often be carved and included jewelled decoration. The slip-on mule was another popular ladies shoe. Shoes became even higher and pointier than before with the stiletto heel reaching its thinnest.

The waist remained a big (or small!) feature throughout the decade, with jackets and dresses shaped accordingly, and the wider 'cinch' style belt introduced to accentuate feminine curves. Capri or cigarette pants (calf-length, slim-legged, high-waisted trousers) were popular and were often worn with a tight sweater. This sexy, rebellious style became known as the 'Sweater Girl' look, and this silhouette would, of course, be incomplete without a conical bra.

Right: This extravagant 50s ball gown is modelled in an ode to Cecil Beaton. It features 12 layers of cotton and tulle.

Top 50s tip

Contrary to popular belief, the 50s shape can suit everyone. A full, high-waisted skirt can hide a multitude of sins. A simple rule for an authentic 50s vintage look: Keep your hemlines just below the knee – never above. Providing the length is correct, it also elongates the calf and makes ankles appear slimmer.

Top 50s tip

Don't be tempted to wear a full petticoat or crinoline underskirt that sticks out past your hemline. This won't add to your 50s look.

Capri Pant Look

Jeni is wearing bright yellow capri pants with a tie waist. Her bark-cloth crop top with pom pom detailing evokes the Tiki style that became fashionable in the 1950s in both clothing and homeware. Her look is finished off with a chiffon headscarf, bamboo hooped earrings and wedge mules.

Full-skirted Look

Jeni is wearing a traditional homemade 50s floral cotton dress with a nipped-in waist, full skirt and cap sleeves. The dress features a 'collar' which cleverly folds down to form a squarer take on a sweetheart neckline. White mesh summer courts, plastic flower earrings and a parasol to shade her complexion complete the look.

The 1960s

'There's so much plastic in this culture that vinyl leopard skin is becoming an endangered synthetic.' Lily Tomlin

Pop music was exploding – from Beatlemania to the Rolling Stones. Boys wanted to be them, and women everywhere wanted to emulate their stylish girlfriends. The 60s left behind all the fuss and constraints of the 40s and 50s; youngsters were outgrowing the 'Make Do and Mend' generation and being frivolous and flirty. Women were more liberated than they had been before – and boy, did it show. Hemlines rose and rose and the miniskirt was born.

Day look shopping list

- Bib fronts
- Monochrome
- Mary Jane shoes
- Pilgrim shoes
- Tights (certainly not seamed stockings!)
- Vinyl accessories
- Trapeze bags
- Square/circular bangles
- Boots

Evening look shopping list

- Sequined mini dresses
- Short baby doll dresses
- Watteau backs (a single back panel that falls unbelted to the hem, like a train)
- Dress suits
- Tailoring
- Matching accessories

Main shapes, looks and influences

Skirt lengths got shorter and shorter throughout the 60s, but it was 1965 when the mini as we know it, sometimes 8 inches above the knee, was born. Mary Quant coined the name apparently in ode to the Mini car. It revolutionised fashion: it was something never seen before; it was bold and brash and it upset your parents. Most importantly, it was something that the average girl could and would wear. High fashion was no longer for the elite.

Lesley Hornby aka Twiggy, Jean Shrimpton and Marianne Faithful were the supermodels of their time. Girls could copy their looks without having to save up for months. The biggest contribution to this fashion revolution was the fact that clothes were so much cheaper to manufacture and distribute across the globe. Biba by Barbara Hulanicki launched in 1963, bringing fashion for the masses by introducing cheap clothing via mail order. She described her ranges as 'Auntie Colours' – blackish mulberries, blueberries, rusts and plums. Gone were the stuffy tailors and there was a big hello to the achingly trendy Kings Road boutiques in Chelsea and Carnaby Street in Soho, London.

The use of plastic was another defining feature. Vinyl (or PVC) was used for coats (especially macs, often with matching rain hats) and even mini dresses. It was also commonly used to make bright chunky jewellery. The demand for fast fashion saw the rise of mass-produced synthetic bags and shoes.

Opposite: A Courrèges navy vinyl coat with white button snaps.

Left: Ladylike accessories and chunky plastic jewellery are very of this era. As are square circle bangles and earrings. If you want to avoid the white go-go boot look, any 60s outfit can be nicely finished off with a Mary Jane-style shoe.

Right: A heavily embellished rhinestone, pearl and bead mini dress.

Opposite top: A scarf tied to a bag can add a personal touch to an otherwise muted outfit.

Opposite below: Pilgrim shoes with a big buckle and flat heel. Wear with white tights for an elongated leg.

What was new?

London was the hub of youth culture and was the epitome of the Swinging Sixties. David Bailey's images of Jean Shrimpton are some of the most iconic images of all time. The film *Blow Up* was said to be based on him. Andy Warhol's pop art was influencing fashion. Amazing prints from Pucci sprung up, all with glorious colours, and weird and wonderful designs were created. Was it fashion or was it art? Some would say both.

The space race dominated the decade. Designers appropriated perceived elements of spacemens' suits – flashes of white, silver and cocoon-like headwear.

The 1960s cannot be talked about without mentioning its two biggest subcultures, the Mods and the Rockers. With motorcycles being the best alternative to the expensive motor car, youngsters were able to be mobile and express themselves in a whole new way. On one hand you had the dapper Modernist boys, who wore Italian bespoke suits and had sharp haircuts; the girls weren't far behind, with their stylish pencil skirts and cardigans. They danced to The Kinks and The Who, or American R&B. On the other hand you had the Rockers, who were less sophisticated in dress but had a very iconic look, combining leather jackets and denim. Both of these looks are still very much around today all over the globe, from Australia to Japan.

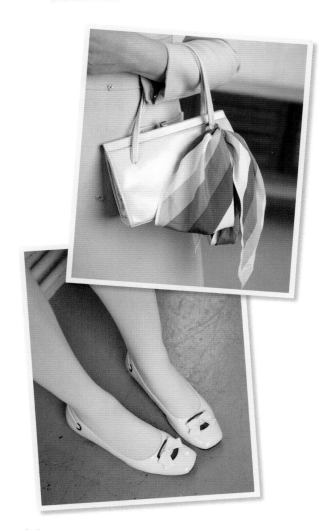

Top 60s tip
Look out for dress suits: a shift dress with matching fitted jacket. Wear together for a Jackie O look, or use as separates.

Informal Look

Alice wears a red and white bib front dress with statement collar. Note the very short skirt and a nod to flower power in its daisy trim. The look is finished with white Mary-Jane shoes and matching square bracelets.

Formal Look

Laura is wearing a Frank Russell for Mansfield coat and a belted two-tone minidress. Frank Russell was a young Jewish tailor from the East End of London who became the 'King of Coats' and sold in high-profile outlets such as Selfridges and Harrods. The cut and the style is very typical of the mid-60s. A white handbag and Pilgrim shoes complete the look.

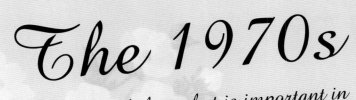

The 1970s

'Over the years I have learned that what is important in a dress is the woman who is wearing it.' Yves Saint Laurent

The rise in air travel, combined with the newly accessible Spanish coast, encouraged holidays abroad. In the United States the Vietnam War had ended, and the new worry was the environment. Climate control had arrived and you could sit in a heated car without a coat. Clothing became multifunctional, moving seamlessly from day to night. Diane von Furstenberg created the simple jersey wrap dress, which could be worn to the office or on the dancefloor.

Day look shopping list

- Tank tops
- Prairie/peasant dresses
- Crochet waistcoats
- Broderie anglaise
- Fringed leather skirts
- Denim
- Polo necks
- Plaited or weaved belts
- Patchwork
- Safari suits
- Pussy bow blouses
- Wide lapels and collars
- Tunics
- Pinafores
- Capes

Evening look shopping list

- Mirror-tile belts
- Cropped, faux-fur jackets
- Lurex
- Low V-necks
- High ruffled necks
- Spaghetti straps
- Halter necks
- Jumpsuits
- Maxi skirts
- Glitter
- Asymmetric tops and dresses

Main shapes, looks and influences

Above and right: It's still pretty easy to find 70s accessories in charity shops. Look out for oversized sunglasses with a squarish frame and long strands of beads. The 70s saw a fondness for mixed-tone leather shoulder bags. Carved bangles were also popular.

The early 70s were all about personal creativity: fashions were either handcrafted, or made to look so. Macramé (woven coloured plastic or straw), crochet and patchwork were popular across the ages. Magazines such as *Over 21* produced a quarterly supplement, *Fashion Workshop*, which combined the latest styles with all the craft techniques needed to make a mirrored belt or knitted sweater.

In America, Bev Hillier's 1971 Art Deco Exhibition reignited a passion for the 30s, which extended to fashions. This is also, importantly, the beginning of the vintage trend as we know it, though it was still known then as 'second hand'. This wasn't recycling out of necessity; it was a lifestyle choice. 'Anything goes' was the attitude towards wearing past fashions and this new 'fad' had a fairly broad appeal.

These trends trickled up to the biggest designers of the day. Ossie Clark and Alice Pollock appropriated the best of 30s eveningwear and turned it into 70s daywear. The bias cut returned, though sleeves became exaggerated versions of their former incarnations. The empire line reappeared. Colours returned to a rich autumnal palette of deep purples, burnt oranges and greens in abstract or mixed floral patterns, though less psycadelic than the previous decade.

The teenage mini skirt trend of the 60s had become a mainstream fashion, worn by mothers and daughters alike. Two new hem lines were introduced: the Midi (A-line and calf length – another nod to the 30s) and the Maxi (a huge volumous creation that came at least to the ankle).

Jeans and trousers were flared, increasing to their largest in the mid-70s. As the decade came to a close, they had slimmed right down to the peg leg shape associated with the 80s, though the high waist remained.

Popular shoes were, of course, platforms, clogs and simple flat sandals from Scholls.

What was new?

In 1976 Yves St Laurent created his peasant look. This is a great summer alternative to the 50s sundress. Tiered skirts were combined with off-the-shoulder blouses inspired by the seventeenth century. Embroidered fabrics from Mexico and appliquéd cheesecloth (gauzelike cotton) were trend staples.

Making a 'Dorothy bag' was a popular way to round off an outfit. This small, pouchlike bag would match your frock, it either came ready-made or was included in the pattern if you were making your own (knitted or cloth).

The 70s cannot be discussed without mentioning disco. Studio 54 and *Saturday Night Fever* were responsible for a million dance floors bristling with static energy. The halter-neck jumpsuit was a major player. Virtually backless, it was equally daringly low at the front.

Left and above: The influences of the 30s can be seen here in Hazel's A-line dress suit in the small raised shoulders, matching buttons and back belt details. The look is brought into the 70s with an oversized Biba silk blouse with balloon sleeves, maroon leather shoulder bag and 70s snakeskin wedges.

Top 70s tip
Buy a lovely wide-brim plain felt hat (as seen on page 81) in a green, dark pink, beige or black and accessorise with a long, thin scarf of your choice, tied around the brim to coordinate with your outfit.

Day Look

Bethan is channelling her inner Goldie Hawn wearing an ankle-length cotton maxi dress with cap sleeves and ric rac trim around the neckline. The look is finished off with sandal clogs, wooden jewellery and a semicircular wicker basket. The dress could be swapped for a kaftan for a more laid-back bohemian look.

Evening Look

Annie is working her photoshoot in a wide-legged halter-neck lycra jumpsuit with a matching tasselled scarf tied at the bodice. The oversized floral print is characteristic of the 70s. The look is finished with a wide brimmed nude felt hat and black platform shoes. For colder nights this would look great with a cropped faux-fur jacket.

The 1980s

"The higher up you go, the more mistakes you are allowed. Right at the top, if you make enough of them, it's considered to be your style." Fred Astaire

The 80s was a decade that took the best of past fashions and reinvented them in an exaggerated, almost cartoon-like manner. It scooped up every major trend and made it bigger, bolder (but, arguably, not better). The drop waist of the 1920s, the peplums of the 1940s and bold floral designs of the 50s were all reclaimed by the decade that fashion forgot. The firm rule for 1980s dressing is big is good, but bigger is better.

Day look shopping list

- Oversized polka dots
- Wide-brimmed hats
- Fingerless lace gloves
- Ra-ra skirts
- Puff-ball skirts
- Shoulder pads in knitwear and blouses
- Jodhpurs
- Stretchy jersey dresses
- Pastels, acids or neons
- Jelly shoes
- Pointy courts
- Collarless jackets
- Double-breasted blazers
- Batwing sleeves

Evening look shopping list

- Strapless prom dresses
- Giant puffed sleeves
- Sequinned jumpsuits
- Ball gowns
- High slits
- Metallic bows
- Chunky gold
- Chain belts
- Clutchbags
- Strong vibrant colours – fuschia, turquoise, bright peach, jade and red

Right: Harriet's wide-brimmed hat and fitted jacket with military-inspired frogging hark back to the style of the late 40s. The jersey material and oversized shoulder pads bring it back to the 80s.

Below: Astral motif detail on a cropped boxy jacket.

Opposite: Accessories were brash: bows, fruit, and studs were popular.

Main shapes, looks and influences

The 1980s saw a stratospheric rise in the number of trends and subcultures. A few are certainly worth a mention; the Club Kids, the New Romantics, the Johnny-come-lately punks left over from the late 70s. Films like *Flashdance* made leggings and cropped sweatshirts fashionable for the young. The MTV generation brought with it the fad for retina scarring neon. Whilst it is tempting to recreate these trends, the looks picked here, I believe, will become future classics for everyday dressing.

Power dressing, inspired by shows such as *Dynasty* and *Dallas,* encouraged the fashion excess that really made for a show-stopping 80s look. Think the biggest shoulder pads you can manage; and diamonds, pearls and gold (fake or real) in oversize shapes, for day and evening. A top-notch power dressing look can be finished off with barely black tights.

The big, and as of yet, unemulated icon of the 1980s was Princess Diana. Credited with reviving the trend for hats, she knew how to dress for the occasion – an art somewhat lost today. Low pumps, wrap dresses and a coy, demure look finished off with a wispy up-do and a large hat.

Clutch bags were popular – the larger, the better. Chanel's quilted chain strap bag was copied a million times over and is still a wardrobe staple today. Costume jewellery saw a huge resurgence in popularity. The chunky novelty items of the

1950s lost any remaining finesse and were left as hunks of gold plate or enamelled in garish primary colours. Astronomy influenced jewellery with stars, moon and planets colliding all over the same brooch or jacket. If it wasn't astral, it was covered in animals or bows.

One of my favourite looks was the matching bag and shoe combo. The 80s saw an increase in popularity of shoes that could be dyed to match your dress, bag, hat or all three at once. Brands such as Charles Jourdan and Roland Cartier created entire accessories ranges in rainbow-bright colours, ready to finish off any outfit.

Below: Power dressing in shiny leopard print. Note again the popularity of 40s detailing in the pleated hip detail.

Whilst disco disappeared in the early 80s, the block colours and sequins of this era clung on for a little while longer in evening wear. The jumpsuit also carried over, though with a tapered leg – as worn by Hazel (left) – and often incorporated a wide bat-winged top.

Daywear was loose and comfortable. If you were not wearing leggings and an oversized jumper, then you were pretty much guaranteed to be wearing a polycotton dress (minimal ironing required) with an elasticated waist. These dresses copied the styles of the late 1940s and early 1950s. Peplums came back in – as seen on this gold dress (left) and red jacket (page 84). Pretty, full-skirted floral dresses, with nipped-in waists sold in abundance from Laura Ashley.

Top 80s tip

How do you differentiate a 50s dress from an 80s dress? This is a serious problem amongst vintage sellers because many are still passing off 80s clothing as earlier, whether knowingly or not. 80s dresses were mass-produced and exaggerated. There just isn't the same attention to detail. Note the lack of darting around the bodice and the absence of the shelf bust. There is a big difference in sleeves. An 80s dress has sleeves a few inches above the elbow, generally straight up and down, compared to the neat cap-sleeve of the 1950s. Take a look at the waist. Is there elastic hidden under that matching fabric belt? If so, I would happily put a punt on it being 80s and not 50s. Also, does that drop-V waist have a piped edging? Run a mile.

Above: Diana epitomised the 80s trend for matching accessories and ladylike outfits.

Day Look

Harriet wears a classic 80s wrap dress by Cockney Rebel, with oversized buttons and polka dots. Note the tulip shape of the skirt exposing the knee. Her white leather shoulder bag and matching court shoe both feature popular gold chain-link detailing. Oversized pearl clip-on earrings complete her look.

Evening Look

Hazel is wearing a full-length white evening dress with side split, plunging V-neck and long sleeves. This look references late 70s disco and is brought back into the 80s by the the sequins and shoulder pads. Plenty of gold jewellery and a matching clutch bag and stiletto sandal turn this in an evening look that could easily be worn today.

Useful Extras

Underwear and shapewear

Having the right underwear can make a huge difference to how clothes sit on you. Don't be afraid, the era of rib-crunching discomfort is long gone. Many fans of vintage and good faux vintage lingerie enjoy the ceremony that comes with attaching your stockings and tweaking your foundation garments, and once you get used to it, it no longer seems quite so tortuous.

A great tragedy about women today is that so many seem to have given up on their waists, or forgotten that they have one at all! The catwalks of the Noughties have given us a trend for hipster jeans and low-slung skirts. Combine this with a fear of a 'muffin top' and we get a too-heavy reliance on baggy clothing. Let us not surrender the natural hourglass curves that make us beautiful – and this is just the shape that vintage fashions highlight so wonderfully! Most girls I know who regularly wear vintage have managed to train their muscles to attain the 'vintage shape' without any recourse to the gym, so let's relocate that fabulous space between our lowest ribs and our hip-bones and put some beautiful curves back on the streets.

Featured here we have two different ways of neatening the waist : the 7" Baby Corset, the one to wear under New Look dresses (opposite); and the Corselette (page 96), introduced in the late 1950s and still worn today. Both are clever reproductions from What Katie Did.

A brief history of underwear

In the 1920s, bras were little more than camisoles, though if you were blessed with larger assets the Symington Side Lacer was a contraption designed to lace up at the sides, enabling ladies to flatten their busts in line with the fashions of the day. This was a big change from the fashions of the previous decade, which pretty much dictated that a woman should squeeze herself into a lace-up corset, boned to draconian proportions. The corset lingered from the 20s to the 50s, but not everyone chose to wear one. The 1930s saw the arrival of the bra almost as we know it, with adjustable back sizes and cup sizes. The construction was not as refined, though, and it was generally made up of three pieces of fabric sewn into a cone.

Contrary to popular belief, the controversial Sweater Girl look first appeared in the 30s. In fact, it was thanks to Lana Turner's appearance in the 1937 film *They Won't Forget*, all pointy boobs and tight cashmere sweater, that the stitched bullet bra enjoyed so much success in the 1950s.

You can forget about the racy colours associated with modern garments. Until the 60s they were functional affairs in a white or peach satin or cotton. Underwiring gave everyone a boost in the 1950s, whilst post-1960 a rounded cup, more commonly associated with current brassières, became de rigeur. In terms of undies, the Tap Pant, as seen on page 95 in black, was popular till the 40s, after which the elasticated baby doll brief was introduced and is still the preferred pant of choice for many women today. Raciness returned in the 1980s with teddies, lace all-in-ones and French knickers.

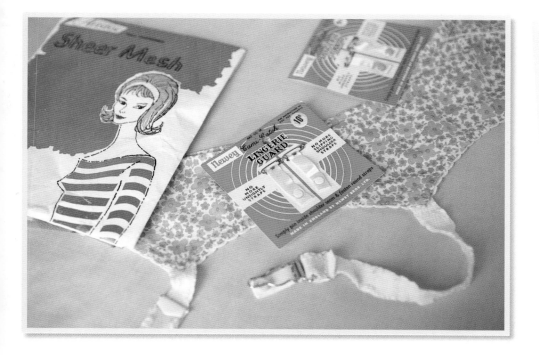

Left: Bra Strap holders (also known as 'lingerie guards'), a packet of 60s stockings and 60s suspender belt.

97

Swimwear

Up until the 1930s bathing suits were generally made out of wool. Ladies' swimsuits comprised what we would consider today to be quite a full covering: a skirt, blouse and even stockings. Annette Kellerman, an Australian professional swimmer and film star, stirred things up in 1907 when she bathed publicly in a 'body stocking' and was promptly arrested for indecency.

The 20s swimsuit still covered the majority of the body, although they tended to be a less complex 'one-piece'.

The 'two-piece' swimsuit first made its appearance in the 30s. At the same time one-pieces and play suits became form-fitting.

In 1946 the 'two-piece' became known as the 'bikini'. It was first introduced by French fashion designer Louis Reard and was named after Bikini Atoll, a nuclear bomb testing site.

50s swimsuits (as pictured here, including one for an infant) were cotton affairs that were not terribly practical for the beach, but embodied the colourful prints and designs of the decade.

By the 1960s swimwear was the more practical garment we use today. It was actually designed with the water in mind!

In the 70s Farah Fawcett single-handedly brought back the craze for the one piece swimsuit or 'maillot'. This time it was high-legged, sexy and tight. This trend lasted well into the 80s.

How to get into vintage clothes

In this section I tell you, literally, how to get into vintage clothes. Over the years I have seen many a frustrated person getting stuck in a frock, only to promptly discard it out of sheer annoyance. With a little bit of careful planning, that same dress would have slipped on easily and fitted a treat. Paying attention to this section will make friends of your local shopkeepers, as a little care results in far less damage to the clothing. (I speak as someone who has had to cut herself out of two dresses because of the zips.)

- Firstly, have a good hard look at the garment. Where does it open?

- Is the belt undone? These are quite often tied onto the garments via the belt loops or even sleeves. Also check for ties and ribbons.

- Check the sides for shorter zips and the back for longer zips. It's not that unusual for a dress to have both.

- Check that the poppers or buttons commonly used to taper long sleeves have been undone.

- Check for built-in slips or corsetry that may bunch up as you put it on.

- Once you are sure everything has been undone, proceed as follows:

- Zips down the back – step into it.

- Zips at the side (common in pre-50s clothes) – put it on over your head.

- If you need to put it over your head, the Number One tip is this: put your hands through the armholes first, then pull over by your head and shoulders, not the other way around. This is the golden rule for not getting stuck in a dress. Most vintage clothing has very little stretch, and 99% of the time you will get your head in and find that you have no room to manoeuvre your arms and shoulders.

- If it doesn't go over your shoulders, don't force it; it certainly will not go over your hips.

- Once in, make sure you have done everything up again, take stock of how it feels and looks (in a full-length mirror) and then make your decision.

How to repair and maintain vintage

Now that you are building yourself your own treasure trove, make you sure you treat it with the same level of care that has allowed it to last this long.

Repairs

Some repairs are easy to do yourself. Others such as replacing zips are better left to the professionals. That said, an old padded sewing box filled with interesting bits and bobs and a pile of items to rescue can make for a very relaxing afternoon.

Avoid where possible cutting hem lines. Instead, fold the fabric no more than twice to the desired length and press well with an iron (on the inside). Then lightly hand-stitch with transparent nylon thread, which is available from all good haberdashers.

If you really must shorten a dress or skirt, keep the spare fabric, don't throw it away. It can be used for making a tie belt if the original is missing or a matching head scarf. Even the smallest scrap can be handy for a repair.

If you come across unpatterned cheap silk scarves, snap them up and keep them for the sewing box. When repairing a tear or moth hole, use a small square of silk to back fabric when darning. The lightweight nature of silk makes it easy to sew through both layers and adds extra reinforcement. This works especially well if you are trying to rescue damaged underarms.

So, what is darning? Well, it's an old-fashioned technique to repair damaged fabric in an area that is away from a seam. Make small neat stitches in silk or wool thread (not cotton) over and around the damaged area, where possible in the same direction of the weave or grain. This can also be applied to patterned fabric so long as you carefully match the threads to the colours.

Washing

The first time you wash a newly acquired vintage treasure can be fairly nerve-wracking, so proceed with caution.

Start off by soaking it in cold water to lift any surface dirt, then gently run the warm tap to see if the colour starts to run. If the sink starts to fill with darks hues of dye, take the garment out and start again on a cooler temperature. This is a common occurrence in crêpe fabric.

If you do feel safe to proceed with the washing machine, always set it to a short run with minimal spin at 30°C. Wash delicate fabrics in a closed cotton pillowcase to stop them being pulled around in the drum. This also works a treat for hosiery and underwear.

Don't machine-wash sequins or glass beads. Even modern ones will melt or discolour. I would also avoid ever machine-washing silk (which goes crispy) or crêpe (which shrinks).

Top tip
For wiffy garments you cannot wash at all, use cheap undiluted vodka in a spritzer bottle and spray the armpits. Works a treat! Removes smells better than dry cleaning.

Stains

- Candlewax – place a piece of brown paper over the wax area. Iron over the paper with a warm iron. Wax melts and gets sealed into the paper! Genius!

- Lipstick – with a knife, scrape away as much lipstick as possible. Apply some washing-up liquid and rub into the stain, then gently dab with water to remove the stain. Repeat if needed.

- Chewing gum – place the item in a plastic bag. Pop the bagged item into freezer. Leave overnight. Remove the item from the bag, and the gum can be scraped clean off!

Drying and pressing

Cotton and linen dries effortlessly and can be ironed without much fear. With anything, start on a very low iron temperature so as not to melt the surface. Certain old synthetic fabrics, including some types of crêpe, will go shiny when heated. Equally, satins may go matte. If in doubt, iron inside out. If you have a serious vintage collection, invest in a home steamer.

If you are hanging washing out on the line, fold the garment at the waist to avoid the damp weight hanging from the shoulders. If it's sunny, cover with an old bit of sheet to avoid bleaching.

Storage

Store everything clean, as moths love dirt. If you can't afford garment bags, place any items for storage in a clean receptacle, high enough to avoid being nibbled by mice.

Avoid hanging garments on metal hangers, as the thinness of the metal can ruin the shape of the shoulder. Invest in padded or wooden hangers. Don't leave your vintage on a rail or cupboard exposed to sunlight, or you will find that the exposed side will fade.

Wrap delicates in pH neutral tissue paper. Most standard paper is acidic and potentially harmful to silk or wool objects.

Labels to look out for

A little label savviness can help you spot fakes and also date garments. If you see an interesting label, a quick internet search can yield wonders. My favourite resource for checking labels is the Vintage Fashion Guild Website. This guide illustrates the changes in fashion labels from the elegant flourish of the 50s and before, to the typography seen today.

Here is a non-exhaustive list of designers, fashion houses and brands you may not know:

- Radley
- Blanes
- Suzy Perrette
- Bill Gibb
- Granny takes a trip
- Alice Pollock

- Clare McCardell
- Janice Wrainright
- Thea Porter
- Swirl
- Droopy and Brown
- Hattie Carnegie

- John Bates for Jean Varon
- Emma Domb
- Ceil Chapman
- Frank Usher
- Jacques Heim
- Lilli Ann
- Alice Edwards
- Susan Small
- Sambo Fashions
- Marshall & Snelgrove

Top tip
Look out for old Laura Ashley labels without the blue circle on them.
These 70s dresses are highly sought-after.

Where to shop

Once you start to look for vintage, you see it everywhere. In the meantime, here are some recommended hunting grounds. You may find if you are a novice that you come home empty-handed from your first few outings. Don't worry, though; it's better to avoid so-so items than to purchase and regret.

• Charity shops – my tip is to go to hospice shops, which often have entire wardrobes donated.

• Vintage shops – these can be expensive, but a good one will be honestly priced. Larger shops may also have too much stock, so if you don't mind rummaging you may find a mislabelled and underpriced item.

• Carboot fares – be prepared to rummage. This is where a good knowledge of print is helpful, as you may catch only a glimpse of fabric peeking out from under a pile of junk.

• Dress agencies – they are very fussy, so good for iconic pieces that will be classics 20 years down the line. Clean and in the best condition, but expect to pay a designer price.

• Auctions – look out for job lots. One good item can redeem an entire lot. Get rid of any undesirables by hosting a 'swishing' or vintage swap shop party.

• If you are a serious collector, put an ad in the paper or online and wait for a house clearance to come up. Quite often, people have no idea what to do with old clothing.

• On the Net – online shopping has become very popular, although eBay is not what it used to be. Etsy does yield interesting items, but I prefer online boutiques. See my list of carefully curated retailers on page 109 for vintage sellers you can trust.

Recommended reading

www.retrochick.co.uk Vintage fashion blogger, whisky drinker, social media flutterby. Blogging about vintage events in pretty frocks, and whatever else she fancies. The authority on Vanity Sizing.

www.pennydreadfulvintage.com Margaret blogs about vintage fashion, and also has a penchant for books, history, London, and sweet things. Check out her shop as well.

www.theatreoffashion.co.uk Authored by a costume historian who doubles as a trend forecaster, this website traces current trends back to their historical precedents, with an emphasis on all that is theatrical in fashion.

www.vintagebrighton.com Celebrates the South Coast's thriving vintage scene.

www.clothesonfilm.com The best website I have found for cinematic referencing.

www.redlegsinsoho.blogspot.com Min writes the most eloquent blog charting her London-based adventures.

www.brightyoungtwins.blogspot.com Two best friends blogging about their time warped existence.

www.landgirl1980.blogspot.com Charly has a penchant for women's history, headscarves and vintage-inspired frockery.

www.rockalily.com Ree Ree blogs about her rockabilly and vintage-themed life.

www.thevintagetraveler.wordpress.com Always ready for a roadtrip, especially in search of vintage treasures or fashion history.

www.jointhestylehighclub.com Lena's personal style blog features vintage news, shopping tips and unusual style muses.

www.theglamourologist.blogspot.com Lucy blogs about the intriguing history of cosmetics, make up & style. One lipstick at a time.

www.perditaspursuits.blogspot.com Perdita's Pursuits is all about having a fabulous time on a modest income, combining thrift, vintage and a little bit of the unusual.

www.straighttalkingmama.blogspot.com A vintage-loving 40-something talking about her life-long love of vintage clothes, homewares, in fact just about everything.

www.thevintageguidetolondon.com The ultimate guide to all things vintage in London.

www.vintagefashionguild.org Home to the best label directory I have seen.

Online vintage shops

www.junosayshello.com Juno Says Hello is a London-based online boutique selling luxury vintage dresses.

www.lovelysvintageemporium.com This is a trend-led vintage fashion and accessories website owned by a magazine fashion stylist and editor.

www.natashabailie.com Natasha sells the best 50s dresses on the net. Also has her own range of 50s-style repro.

www.lovemissdaisy.com Mother and daughter-run boutique full of beautiful cherry-picked pieces from around the world. Stockist of vintage wedding dresses.

www.corinacorina.com Well priced vintage and reworked clothing.

Acknowledgements

This book is dedicated to Margaret Chester and Jean Thompson, my grandmothers, who inspire me every day.

I am lucky to have a group of very talented friends who helped me make this book. They are nearly all vintage experts in their own right, so, where possible, I have included their blogs and websites for additional inspiration and reading.

Models (in order of appearance)

Fleur De Guerre (www.diaryofavintagegirl.com)

Annie Smith (www.annieanniepancake.blogspot.com)

Teowa

Gemma King (www.bakedoandmend.blogspot.com)

Kezia Argue

Lisa Prest (www.snoodlebugvintage.blogspot.com)

Rachel Baynton

Jennifer Siggs (www.jennyjenny-yesterdaygirl.blogspot.com)

Alice Saggers

Laura Lee

Hazel Holtham (www.ragandbow.com)

Bethan Gwenllian Garland (www.thevintagemafia.com)

Annie Andrews (www.ringoftheswing.wordpress.com)

Harriet Thompson

Stockists

Heyday Vintage Style – Excellent wearable reproduction garments, including Fleur's trousers. (www.heydayonline.co.uk)

What Katy Did – Purveyors of the finest repro and faux vintage underwear, as seen on Annie and the best dressed legs in town. (www.whatkatiedid.com)

Rag and Bow, The Vintage Roaming Store – excellent on-trend items, hand-picked by owner and model Hazel. (www.ragandbow.com)

Sharon and her team for The Shop have every kind of vintage accessory under the sun. (www.theshopvintage.wordpress.com)

The Vintage Emporium have, without a doubt, the best collection of pre-50s dresses in the world (Teowa's 20's day dress). (www.vintageemporiumcafe.com)

Fine jewellery (1920–1960) and all Art Deco pieces thanks to Natalie at Passionate About Vintage (www.passionateaboutvintage.co.uk)

Reproduction shoes for dancing and style (as seen on Fleur) from Remix. (www.remixvintageshoes.com)

Fine reproduction tailoring from Puttin' on the Ritz (Gemma's Reproduction suit). (www.puttin-on-the-ritz.net)

Hunky Dory Vintage: hand selected post-40s European clothing experts and generally lovely people. (www.hunkydoryvintage.com)

Dead Man's Glory Vintage for a really amazing and eclectic selection of 20th century design. (ww.deadmansglory.co.uk)

Research

Liz Tregenza (www.queen-tree.blogspot.com)

Gemma Seager (www.retrochick.co.uk)

Akeela Bhattay (www.akeela.co.uk)

Lucy Wills (www.glamourkitten.com)

Loans

Josefine for the loan of the flapper dress
   (www.historiesanciennes.blogspot.com)

Locations

The Vintage Emporium Tea Rooms
   (www.vintageemporiumcafe.com)

The Love Shake (www.theloveshake.co.uk)

Time for Tea (www.timefortea.org.uk)

First Option studio (www.studiohirefirstoption.com)

BASE @ The Shoreditch.com (info@jjlocations.co.uk)

Styling Assistants

Mared Edwards (www.marededwards.blogspot.com)

Amy Tapsfield

Jo Stobbs

Octavia Austin

Hair and make-up

Amanda and Natasha at Lipstick and Curls
   (www.lipstickandcurls.co.uk)

Photography

Christina Wilson (www.christinawilson.co.uk)

Additional photography

Celine Chaplin, Ken Sparkes and Anthony Lycett.

Thanks to Katherine Higgins, Angel Adoree, Olly and Jess from
the Vintage Emporium, Ian and Ian from Hunky Dory Vintage,
Emily Preece-Morrison at Anova and Rebecca Winfield for all
your help and support. Thank you to The Vintage Mafia for being
the best friends a gal could wish for.

Picture credits

Images ©: 23: Blue Lantern Studio / Corbis; 31: V&A
Images / Alamy; 33T: AF archive / Alamy;
33B: Pictorial Press Ltd / Alamy; 43: Mary Evans
Picture Library / National Magazine Company
53: Jeff Morgan 09 / Alamy; 57: Ken Sparkes;
63: V&A Images / Alamy; 73: Condé Nast Archive/
Corbis; 83: Condé Nast Archive / Corbis; 87: Glenn
Harvey / Alamy; 100: Celine Chapman;
108: Anthony Lycett

First published in the United Kingdom in 2012 by

PAVILION BOOKS

10 Southcombe Street, London W14 0RA

An imprint of Anova Books Company Ltd

"Style Me Vintage" is a registered trademark of Anova Books Ltd.

Text © Naomi Thompson, 2012
Design and layout © Anova Books, 2012
Photography © Anova Books, 2012,
except those images listed in Credits p.111

Commissioning editor: Emily Preece-Morrison
Cover and concept design: Georgina Hewitt
Layout: Laura Woussen
Photographer: Christina Wilson
Hair and make-up: Lipstick and Curls
Stylist: Naomi Thompson www.vintagesecret.com
Models: Fleur De Guerre, Annie Smith, Teowa, Gemma King, Kezia Argue, Lisa Prest, Rachel Baynton,
Jennifer Siggs, Alice Saggers, Laura Lee, Hazel Holtham, Bethan Garland, Annie Andrews, Harriet Thompson
Copy editor: Caroline Curtis

ISBN: 9781862059368

A CIP catalogue record for this book is available from the British Library.

10 9 8 7 6 5 4 3 2

Colour reproduction by Rival Colour Ltd., UK
Printed and bound by G. Canale & C.SpA, Italy